Superstar Cars

Jaguar

Robin Johnson

CRABTREE
Publishing Company
www.crabtreebooks.com

Superstar Cars

Author: Robin Johnson
Publishing plan research and development:
   Sean Charlebois, Reagan Miller
   Crabtree Publishing Company
Editor: Sonya Newland
Proofreader: Molly Aloian
Editorial director: Kathy Middleton
Project coordinator and prepress technician: Margaret Salter
Print coordinator: Katherine Berti
Series consultant: Petrina Gentile
Cover design: Ken Wright
Design: Balley Design Limited
Photo research: Amy Sparks

Photographs:
Alamy: Stuart Hickling: p. 17; Alvey & Towers Picture Library: p. 22; Bob Masters Classic Car Images: p. 23; travelib prime: p. 24; W Motorsport Images: p. 36; Colin C. Hill: pp. 36–37; Paul Debois: p. 45; William Jackson: p. 48–49
Corbis: Martyn Goddard: p. 5; Bettmann: p. 18; H. Armstrong Roberts/ClassicStock: p. 28; Bruce Benedict/Transtock: p. 38, 40–41; Leo Mason: p. 44–45; Schlegelmilch: p. 49
Jaguar: p. 4, 6, 7, 8, 10–11, 50, 51, 52, 52–53, 54, 56–57, 57, 58–59
Motoring Picture Library: p. 1, 9, 13, 14–15, 15, 16, 19, 20–21, 21, 26, 27, 28–29, 30, 38–39, 41, 43, 46–47, 47
Shutterstock: front cover; Adriano Castelli: p. 55

Library and Archives Canada Cataloguing in Publication

Johnson, Robin (Robin R.)
   Jaguar / Robin Johnson.

(Superstar cars)
Includes index.
Issued also in an electronic format.
ISBN 978-0-7787-2143-7 (bound).--ISBN 978-0-7787-2150-5 (pbk.)

   1. Jaguar automobile--Juvenile literature.
I. Title. II. Series: Superstar cars

TL215.J3J64 2011   j629.222'2   C2010-905630-2

Library of Congress Cataloging-in-Publication Data

Johnson, Robin (Robin R.)
   Jaguar / Robin Johnson.
     p. cm. -- (Superstar cars)
   Includes index.
   ISBN 978-0-7787-2150-5 (pbk. : alk. paper) --
   ISBN 978-0-7787-2143-7 (reinforced library binding : alk. paper) --
   ISBN 978-1-4271-9548-7 (electronic (pdf))
   1. Jaguar automobile--Juvenile literature. I. Title. II. Series.

TL215.J3J64 2010
629.222'2--dc22
                              2010034935

Crabtree Publishing Company

Printed in the U.S.A./102010/SP20100915

www.crabtreebooks.com   1-800-387-7650

Published in Canada
Crabtree Publishing
616 Welland Ave.
St. Catharines, ON
L2M 5V6

Published in the United States
Crabtree Publishing
PMB 59051
350 Fifth Avenue, 59th Floor
New York, New York 10118

Published in the United Kingdom
Crabtree Publishing
Maritime House
Basin Road North, Hove
BN41 1WR

Published in Australia
Crabtree Publishing
386 Mt. Alexander Rd.
Ascot Vale (Melbourne)
VIC 3032

>> Contents

Chapter 1

One Cool Cat ≫≫≫≫≫≫≫≫≫≫

A jaguar is a big, wild cat. It is strong and muscular but moves with speed, grace, and agility. It is the ideal name for a company that produces sleek and powerful cars. The Jaguar name has been attached to luxury automobiles for 75 years, and during that time, Jaguar Cars Ltd. has earned a reputation for swift, stylish, and sophisticated cars.

Grace, space, and pace

Jaguar has always strived to produce high-quality, high-value automobiles that inspire and impress. The company motto of "Grace, Space, and Pace" underpins every aspect of the Jaguar design process. It has led to the creation of many **iconic** cars, such as the 1960s Jaguar E-Type. The E-Type sports car became a symbol of the fast and free lifestyle of that generation.

Stylish sports cars

The E-Type is just one of several fast and glamorous sports cars for which Jaguar has become world famous. The XK120 and XK8 models combined grace with superior handling, while the XJ220 showed the world that **supercars** were not just for superheroes. Jaguar's powerfully stylish sports cars have driven the company's success since the early twentieth century.

The classic XJ sedan has come to exemplify the sophistication and style of Jaguar cars.

Sophisticated sedans

Jaguar has also produced many fine luxury **sedans**, such as the Mark VII and X-Type models. A sedan is a passenger car with four doors and a back seat. The XJ model has been Jaguar's **flagship** sedan for more than four decades.

Racing roadsters

Jaguar has been as successful on the racetrack as it has been on city streets. Between 1951 and 1990, Jaguar won the **prestigious** 24 Hours of Le Mans an impressive seven times. That's more than any other British car manufacturer in the enduring history of the race. The Jaguar C-Type, D-Type, XJR series, and other racing models have set the pace on racetracks around the world.

■■➡

The iconic E-Type created a powerful image of the Jaguar car company that endures today.

Made in England

Jaguar vehicles have always been made with pride in England. British cars are known all over the world for their luxury, elegance, and style. Rolls-Royce, Bentley, and Aston Martin are some of the other classy car brands that were born in Britain.

FPB 255B

Founding fathers

The Jaguar car company was formed on September 4, 1922. It was originally called Swallow Sidecar Company. Swallow Sidecars was founded by William Lyons and William Walmsley in Blackpool, England. The two Williams were friends and motorcycle fans. At first, their company made only **sidecars** for motorcycles. William Lyons soon wanted to expand the business and build motorcars, however. In 1935, he bought out William Walmsley and became sole owner of the fast-growing company.

The Lyons king

William Lyons devoted his life to Jaguar cars. He was a careful businessman who ran the company until 1967. During that time, William designed nearly every car produced by Jaguar. He built up his company by creating stylish, luxurious vehicles that offered drivers high performance and good value.

In 1956, William Lyons was knighted for his contribution to the British auto industry and for the successful sale of his cars around the world. In 1972, Sir William retired from Jaguar Cars. He passed away in 1985.

Jaguars are manufactured at the Castle Bromwich Assembly plant in Birmingham, United Kingdom, and in the Halewood Body and Assembly plant in Liverpool, United Kingdom.

Jaguar today

Today, Jaguar cars—which are often called simply Jags—are designed in state-of-the-art facilities around the world. They are assembled with care in the United Kingdom. There, skilled craftspeople use the latest technologies to build award-winning vehicles, such as the new Jaguar XF, XK, and XJ models.

AMAZING FACTS

Honor roll

Jaguar has been honored with countless awards since it began crafting automobiles. It has been recognized for the performance, styling, and comfort of both its sports cars and sedans. The Jaguar E-Type even won first prize in a beauty contest!

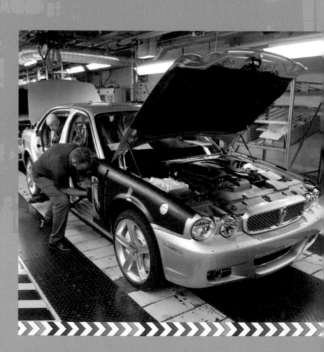

Sir William Lyons, the founder of the company, is often called "Mr. Jaguar."

Star power

Jaguars have been featured in many popular movies. Austin Powers was the picture of cool in his 1961 custom E-Type sports car. A 1997 XK8 made a memorable appearance in the 2000 thriller *Memento*. A Mark VIII sedan stole the show in the 1958 Alfred Hitchcock film *Vertigo*.

JAGUAR

Chapter 2

>A Legend is Born>>>>>>>>>

Jaguar Cars Ltd. roared to life in the 1920s. After several years of rebuilding and recovering from World War I, London and other cities began to prosper. People listened to jazz music, danced, and celebrated changing attitudes and lifestyles. New technologies showed people the possibilities of the modern world. They liked what they saw.

From sidecars to sedans

Swallow Sidecars had begun making cars by 1927. During the late 1920s and early 1930s, the company produced a variety of luxury sedans. In 1931, Swallow Sidecars introduced the SS1 model. The SS1 was a stylish sports car that became the first iconic Jaguar.

The SS1

With its low, sweeping design and strikingly long hood, the SS1 was an instant classic. The car's interior was equally stunning. It was **opulent**, with leather and wood trim. Although the SS1 was praised for its comfort and handling, its top speed was only 75 mph (121 km/h). What the SS1 lacked in power, though, it made up for in price. The 1932 base model cost only around US$450—about one-third the cost of a similar Bentley.

FXD 293

Jaguar is born

In 1933, Swallow Sidecars was renamed
SS Cars Ltd. to reflect the company's
new focus on automobile production.
Two years later, the first Jaguar was
born. The Jaguar SS 100 was an eye-
catching two-seat sports car. It is
considered by many to be one of the
most attractive cars that Jaguar ever
produced. The car's long, muscular
body and graceful curves were
decidedly catlike. It was the ideal
car to introduce the name and create
the image of Jaguar.

An early sidecar built by Swallow
Sidecars—the company that
evolved into Jaguar Cars Ltd.

Swallow Sidecars sold some 4,200
of the popular SS1 sports cars from
1932 to 1936.

The Great Depression

The Great Depression was a period
of severe economic hardship in the
1930s. It affected nearly every country
in the world. Many people struggled
to support their families and a lot
of companies went out of business.
Sir William Lyons kept his company
alive, however, by making cars
that offered both incredible
beauty and value.

▶▶ King of the jungle

The Jaguar SS 100 was no kitty cat, however. With a 3.5-liter six-cylinder engine, it had speed and power to spare. True to its name, the SS 100 reached top speeds of 100 mph (160 km/h). It could accelerate from 0 to 60 mph (97 km/h) in less than 11 seconds! Only 308 Jaguar SS 100 models were produced, making the cars extremely rare—and valuable—today. The SS 100 model originally sold for about US$2,000. Today, models in good condition sell for US$150,000 to US$250,000!

World War II

On September 1, 1939, World War II began. German forces invaded Poland and started what would become the biggest and deadliest conflict in history. Soon, nearly every country in the world—including Britain—was involved in the war. Factories everywhere were used to make weapons and other war supplies instead of producing automobiles and luxury goods. Production of Jaguars and other cars stopped for a long time and only began again when the war ended in 1945.

The Jaguar SS 100 was the cat's pajamas! That expression, very popular at the time, meant that something was really great.

Same name

SS Cars had begun to make a name for itself around the world. Unfortunately, another organization with the same initials was also becoming famous at the same time. The Schutzstaffel—known simply as the SS—was Adolf Hitler's security organization in Nazi Germany. The SS committed many cruel acts before and during World War II. The SS Car company changed its name so it would not be associated with the deadly Schutzstaffel.

ERB 290

The war effort

During World War II, SS Cars produced sidecars for army vehicles. The company also learned how to design and build aircraft—knowledge that helped them make powerful new cars after the war. At night, the workers had firewatch duty on the roof of the factory, which involved checking for and reporting fires caused by air raids on the city. Sir William Lyons and a team of engineers began planning a new engine during their long nights on firewatch. Their discussions led to the famous XK engine that was produced by the company after the war.

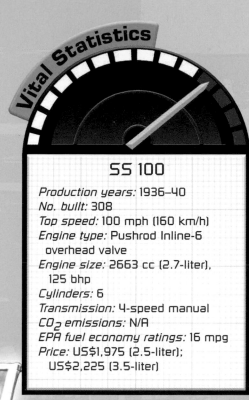

Vital Statistics

SS 100

Production years: 1936–40
No. built: 308
Top speed: 100 mph (160 km/h)
Engine type: Pushrod Inline-6 overhead valve
Engine size: 2663 cc (2.7-liter), 125 bhp
Cylinders: 6
Transmission: 4-speed manual
CO_2 emissions: N/A
EPA fuel economy ratings: 16 mpg
Price: US$1,975 (2.5-liter); US$2,225 (3.5-liter)

▶▶ A new breed of cars

In 1945, SS Cars was renamed Jaguar Cars Ltd. Sir William Lyons chose the name Jaguar because it reflected the speed, power, grace, and agility of the company's new breed of cars. They came up with a logo that would encapsulate these qualities.

The war is over!

World War II ended on September 2, 1945. London had been devastated by the conflict. Many homes, factories, and other buildings had been destroyed by aerial bombs. After the war, people began to slowly rebuild the city. They also reorganized factory production, which had been dedicated to the war effort for several years.

The finer things

While England had been hurt by World War II, the United States had prospered. People there wanted—and could afford—some of life's finer things. Jaguar answered the call with the XK120 sports car and the Mark VII sedan. Jaguar **exported** most of these stylish cars to North America.

A pouncing jaguar became the face of the luxury car company. It was attached to the hoods of early Jaguar models.

XK120

In 1948, Jaguar introduced the glamorous XK120 **roadster**. The XK120 was an instant sensation. The car's stunning looks and superb lines caught the attention of people everywhere. Powered by the groundbreaking Jaguar XK engine, the XK120 was not just another pretty face, however. Its speed—which reached 120 mph (193 km/h) and inspired its name—made the XK120 the world's fastest **production car** at the time.

Passing the test

The XK120 was originally built as a test car for Jaguar's XK engine. Only about 200 XK120 cars were to be made for testing purposes. The XK120 became so popular, however, that Sir William Lyons decided to put the car into production. Jaguar went on to sell more than 12,000 of the stylish sports cars!

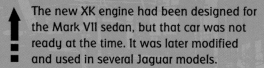

The new XK engine had been designed for the Mark VII sedan, but that car was not ready at the time. It was later modified and used in several Jaguar models.

XH engine

The Jaguar XK was an innovative dual overhead camshaft (DOHC) inline six-cylinder engine. It produced 160 brake horsepower when it was first introduced in 1949. The XK engine was later modified and used in several Jaguar models, including the triumphant C-Type and D-Type racecars. It remained in production until 1992.

>> Mass appeal

The first 240 XK120 roadsters were built by hand. They had wooden frames covered with aluminum panels. Later, **mass-produced** XK120 models had pressed-steel bodies instead of aluminum. The new versions maintained aluminum doors, hoods, and trunk lids, however. They also kept the stylish good looks of the original model.

In 1951, a **coupe** model was added to production. Jaguar later followed up the successful XK120 sports car with the XK140 and XK150 models.

Vital Statistics

XK120

Production years: 1948–54
No. built: 12,055
Top speed: 120 mph (193 km/h)
Engine type: Dual overhead camshaft (DOHC) Inline-6 XK
Engine size: 3442 cc (3.4 liter), 160 bhp
Cylinders: 6
Transmission: 4-speed manual
CO_2 emissions: N/A
EPA fuel economy ratings: N/A
Price: US$4,000

In 1950, Jaguar began to mass-produce the XK120 to meet the high demand for the car.

Mark of luxury

The Mark V was Jaguar's first post-war sedan. The large and luxurious automobile was introduced in 1948. It was offered as a four-door sedan or two-door drophead coupe. A drophead coupe is a convertible, or a car with a roof that can be removed or folded down. Both models had traditional Jaguar styling, including four round headlights and a large vertical chrome grille. They also had spacious, plush interiors and comfort to spare.

Independence day

The Mark V was the first Jaguar sedan to have independent front suspension, meaning that, rather than being connected by a rigid axle, the front wheels move separately from each other. By moving separately, one wheel is not affected by bumps or movements on the other wheel. This new suspension gave the Mark V a smoother, more comfortable ride than Jaguar's previous sedans.

 Only about 1,000 Mark V drophead coupes were made in total. As a result, they are highly prized by car collectors today.

Mark speed

The Mark V had a top speed of 91 mph (146 km/h). It took more than 20 seconds for the big car to accelerate from 0 to 60 mph (97 km/h)! This might not seem too speedy today, but like all Jaguar cars, the Mark V was considered fast at the time.

🏁 AMAZING FACTS

Missing the Mark

Although the Mark VII followed the Mark V, its number did not! At the time, there was another luxury car called the Bentley Mark VI already on the roads. Sir William Lyons decided to skip a number and call the updated sedan the Mark VII instead.

≫ Lucky number 7

Three years later, Jaguar replaced the Mark V with the more powerful Mark VII. Car lovers around the world cheered for the new model. The popular Mark VII featured the same engine used in the XK120 sports car. The Jaguar XK engine allowed the Mark VII to reach speeds over 100 mph (160 km/h), which was remarkable for such a large sedan. It could accelerate from 0 to 60 mph (97 km/h) in less than 14 seconds—a great improvement over the Mark V.

Browns Lane

To meet demand for the popular Mark VII and XK120 models, Jaguar Cars moved into a larger factory in 1951. The factory—located on Browns Lane in the city of Coventry, England—became Jaguar's main production plant until 1998. A portion of this historic plant is still used today for the Jaguar Heritage Museum.

Jaguar unveiled the Mark VII sedan at the 1950 British International Motor Show.

The Mark VII is still popular with collectors all over the world. This Mark VII is being raced around the track at the Goodwood Festival of Speed in the UK.

Streamlined sedan

The design of the Mark VII was updated, too. It had a more modern, **streamlined** look than the model it replaced. Jaguar continued the sedan series throughout the 1950s with the Mark VIII (1956–58) and Mark IX (1959–61) models. However, None of the later models could match the popularity or sales of the original Mark VII.

Vital Statistics

Mark VII

Production years: 1951–56
No. built: 30,969
Top speed: 100 mph (160 km/h) 1951–54; 104 mph (167 km/h) 1954–56
Engine type: Dual overhead camshaft (DOHC) Inline-6 XK
Engine size: 3442 cc (3.4 liter) 160 bhp (1951–54); 190 bhp (1954–56)
Cylinders: 6
Transmission: 4-speed manual; 3-speed automatic optional from 1953
CO_2 emissions: N/A
EPA fuel economy ratings: 17.6 mpg
Price: US$4,000–US$4,600

⚑ AMAZING FACTS

Fit for a queen

The Jaguar Mark VII was fit for a queen—or a queen's mother! Queen Elizabeth the Queen Mother used a 1955 Mark VII for nearly 20 years. The sedan was painted the deep red color used for royal state cars.

17

⟩⟩ The 1950s

During the 1950s, people began buying cars as never before. In the United States, the economy was booming. People bought big houses and filled them with televisions and shiny new appliances. They drove big, flashy cars with long tail fins and colorful paint jobs. Cars like the Ford Thunderbird and Chevrolet Bel Air were popular. In Europe, however, the economy was still recovering from World War II. And the road to recovery was long and bumpy.

In America, big, gas-guzzling cars were all the rage in the 1950s. In Britain, however, the oil embargo meant small cars were more popular.

Running out of gas

In 1956, the Suez Crisis occurred. This was a war fought by Britain, France, and Israel against Egypt. One result of the war was an oil **embargo**—certain oil-producing nations refused to sell their vital product to Britain.

The embargo led to gas **rationing** in Britain. As a result, sales of large, gas-guzzling vehicles decreased. Small, basic, inexpensive cars—such as the Volkswagen Beetle and the Austin Mini—were soon crowding London streets. Sir William Lyons realized that to stay competitive, Jaguar must produce smaller cars that could be manufactured in large numbers.

Small sedan

In 1955, Jaguar introduced a small but elegant sedan. The Mark I—known simply as the Jaguar 2.4-liter or 3.4-liter at the time—offered high performance in a compact body. The Mark I was about one foot (30 cm) shorter and narrower than the Mark VII. The smaller size of the Mark I made it a big hit both at home and overseas. It quickly outsold Jaguar's larger sedans. Four years later, Jaguar introduced the equally popular Mark II sedan.

The Mark II was offered with a variety of engine sizes—2.4, 3.4, and 3.8 liters. This and the Mark I were smaller than previous Jaguars.

AMAZING FACTS

Model cars

The name "Mark" means "model," and carmakers use it to identify different builds of cars. Jaguar built many cars in many different models!

Chapter 3
The Swinging Sixties »»»»»

In the 1960s, London was the center of a cultural revolution. Young people celebrated their freedom of expression. They rebelled against rules and authority. They listened to new rock bands. Women wore miniskirts and bikinis. Men wore bell-bottom jeans and grew their hair long.

■ The E-Type's glass-covered headlights, above-the-bumper lights, and chrome-spoked wheels were universally admired.

🏁 AMAZING FACTS

No contest

The Jaguar E-Type won first prize in a beauty contest! In 2008, a British newspaper called *The Daily Telegraph* conducted a survey of "The 100 Most Beautiful Cars of All Time." The stunning Jaguar E-Type received nearly four times as many votes as any other beauty—including the Jaguar XK120, which placed third on the list.

Meeting demand

The British economy had, for the most part, recovered from World War II. People began spending money again. They wanted things that were modern, stylish, and fun. Jaguar Cars had just what they were looking for.

The most beautiful car

In 1961, Jaguar introduced the glamorous E-Type model. The E-Type—known as the XKE in North America—was a stunning **grand tourer**, a two-seat sports car made for driving long distances in comfort. The E-Type's curved, tubular body was unlike any car ever made before. In fact, Enzo Ferrari, founder of Ferrari racecars, called the E-Type "the most beautiful car ever built." The E-Type was fast, affordable, and wildly popular.

Inside the E-Type, leather bucket seats and an aluminum-trimmed console added an air of sophistication to the stylish car.

The British Invasion

"The British Invasion" is a term used to describe the popularity of British rock bands such as The Beatles, The Rolling Stones, and The Who in the United States during the 1960s. Jaguar Cars Ltd. launched a similar invasion of the American auto industry. About 60 percent of Jaguar E-Type cars were shipped to the United States.

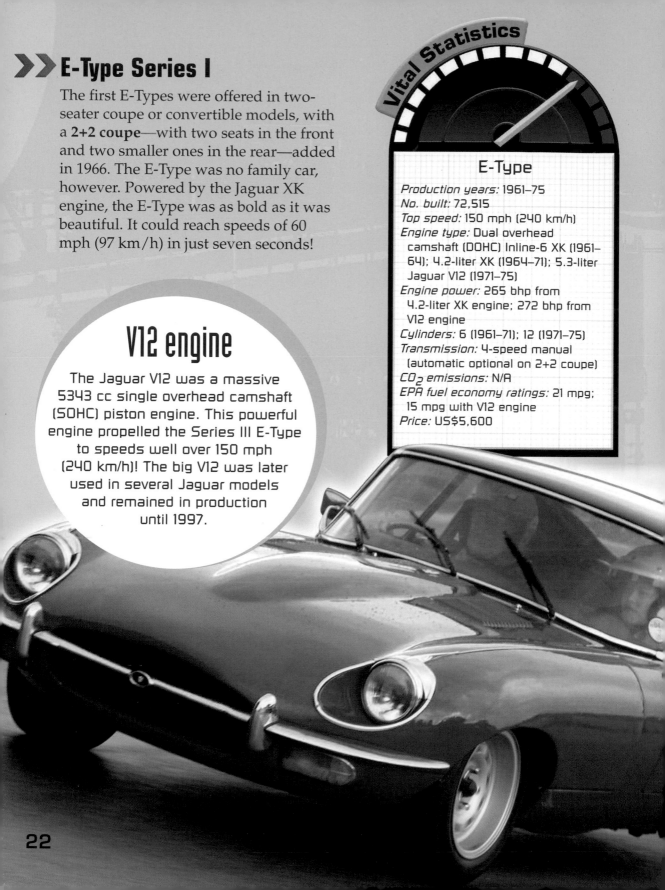

≫ E-Type Series I

The first E-Types were offered in two-seater coupe or convertible models, with a **2+2 coupe**—with two seats in the front and two smaller ones in the rear—added in 1966. The E-Type was no family car, however. Powered by the Jaguar XK engine, the E-Type was as bold as it was beautiful. It could reach speeds of 60 mph (97 km/h) in just seven seconds!

V12 engine

The Jaguar V12 was a massive 5343 cc single overhead camshaft (SOHC) piston engine. This powerful engine propelled the Series III E-Type to speeds well over 150 mph (240 km/h)! The big V12 was later used in several Jaguar models and remained in production until 1997.

Vital Statistics

E-Type

Production years: 1961–75
No. built: 72,515
Top speed: 150 mph (240 km/h)
Engine type: Dual overhead camshaft (DOHC) Inline-6 XK (1961–64); 4.2-liter XK (1964–71); 5.3-liter Jaguar V12 (1971–75)
Engine power: 265 bhp from 4.2-liter XK engine; 272 bhp from V12 engine
Cylinders: 6 (1961–71); 12 (1971–75)
Transmission: 4-speed manual (automatic optional on 2+2 coupe)
CO_2 emissions: N/A
EPA fuel economy ratings: 21 mpg; 15 mpg with V12 engine
Price: US$5,600

E-Type Series II and III

Several design changes altered the look of the Series II E-Type, which was introduced in 1969. For safety reasons, the car's stylish glass headlight covers were removed. The signal and taillights were enlarged and moved below the bumpers, which were also enlarged. In 1971, further changes were made to the iconic car. The Series III E-Type featured a large front grille and subtle wheel arches. It also had a "V12" badge on the back of the car, which proudly announced its powerful new 5.3-liter 12-cylinder engine.

A 1973 Jaguar Series III E-Type roadster. This model was capable of speeds exceeding 150 mph (240 km/h).

Muscling in

In the 1960s, **muscle-car** fever spread across the United States. Muscle cars—such as the Ford Mustang, Chevrolet Camaro, and Dodge Charger—were popular for both street use and **drag racing**. Jaguar muscled in on the American muscle car competition with its Series III E-Type model and hefty V12 engine.

The Series 1 E-Type was produced between 1961 and 1968. At first, they were produced only for export, but it wasn't long before they were sold in the UK, too.

What a lightweight!

A dozen "Lightweight" E-Type racing models were made from 1963 to 1964. These cars—which used a lightweight aluminum **alloy** in their construction—achieved an incredible 300 bhp of power. Today, car collectors pay top dollar to own one of these rare beauties.

>> A growing company

In 1960, Jaguar purchased a luxury car manufacturer called Daimler Motor Company. Jaguar kept the Daimler **marque**, or brand name, and used it for their most expensive and luxurious sedans. In 1966, Jaguar Cars Ltd. merged with British Motor Corporation. The new, larger company was called British Motor Holdings. Two years later, another merger resulted in a new owner of the Jaguar marque—the British Leyland Motor Corporation.

The Jaguar image

"Jaguar isn't a car, it's an image—an image of what was so great with British cars that were quite like us in the '60s: adventurous, rebellious, and independent."

Phil Edmonston, "Lemon-Aid 2010 New Cars and Trucks"

Big business

While Jaguar continued to grow throughout the 1960s, so did the international auto industry. American car companies in particular were thriving. In 1964, Chevrolet sold more than one million Impala models in the United States—a record that still stands today. Other luxury cars, such as the Ford Galaxie and Plymouth Fury, were also big sellers. These spacious, upscale models offered buyers powerful engines, modern styling, and affordable luxury.

The Jaguar Mark X was nearly 17 feet (five m) long! The oversized sedan proved that bigger is not always better, even for American customers.

X marks the spot

In 1961, Jaguar introduced the Mark X. The large and luxurious sedan was made to be sold in the United States. It was the widest production car that Jaguar had ever built, measuring 6.4 feet (1.9 m) across! Unfortunately, the oversized sedan—which was renamed the 420G in 1966—was not a big seller. Even in the American market, many buyers felt that the Mark X was simply too large for them.

The Mark X was the first Jaguar sedan with independent rear suspension. It was also the first of many Jaguar vehicles to feature four round headlights set in a rounded front fender.

›› XJ6

The XJ6, on the other hand, was just the right size. Introduced in 1968, the full-size luxury four-door sedan had style, grace, and plenty of space. Its distinctive profile—now associated with the Jaguar brand—made the XJ6 instantly recognizable. With features such as leather upholstery, power-assisted steering, and optional air conditioning, the XJ6 offered class and comfort. With a six-cylinder engine—for which the car was named—it also had plenty of power.

XJ6

Production years: 1968–73
No. built: 82,126
Top speed: 124 mph (200 km/h)
Engine type: 2.8-liter or 4.2-liter dual overhead camshaft (DOHC) Inline-6 XK
Engine size: 2790 cc (2.8 liter), 245 bhp
Cylinders: 6
Transmission: 4-speed manual; 3-speed automatic
CO_2 emissions: N/A
EPA fuel economy ratings: 16 mpg
Price: approx. US$4,300 (2.8-liter); US$5,800 (4.2-liter)

What's in a name?

The name XJ stands for "Experimental Jaguar." It was a code name given to the model while it was being designed and engineered. The name stuck, and generations of drivers have now enjoyed a successful Jaguar "experiment."

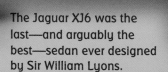

The Jaguar XJ6 was the last—and arguably the best—sedan ever designed by Sir William Lyons.

XJ Series I

For drivers who wanted even more power, the XJ12 model was also offered. With a 5.3-liter V12 engine, the XJ12 reached speeds of around 140 mph (225 km/h). At the time, it was the fastest four-seat car in the world. For those who wanted more luxury, the XJ6 was also offered as an upscale version called the Daimler Sovereign. The XJ12 was available as the elegant Daimler Double-Six. Together, the four models made up a group of Jaguar cars that were later called Series I.

 DS420s—also called Daimler Limousines—were elegant, spacious, and always handmade.

AMAZING FACTS

Final journey

The body of Diana, Princess of Wales, was carried to rest in a Daimler Limousine after her death in a car accident in 1997.

XJ Series II and III

The XJ6 model received many design changes over the years. For example, higher rubber bumpers were added and the size of the front grille was decreased. The modified XJ6 models were released as Series II (1973–79) and Series III (1979–92) versions. Other changes and improvements were made in later years. In fact, the popular XJ series is still produced today!

Fit for a king

For the ultimate in luxury, Jaguar offered the Daimler DS420. DS420s were elegant limousines made from 1968 to 1992. DS420s were often used by the British royal family for funerals, weddings, and other matters of state. Many DS420s were modified and made into **hearses**.

Chapter 4

>The Legend Continues>>>>>>

In the past four decades, the auto industry has shifted away from large, gas-guzzling vehicles toward more practical and fuel-efficient cars. In North America, the trend began with the oil crisis.

Don't be fuelish!

In 1973, a series of conflicts resulted in an oil embargo. Arab nations refused to sell oil to the United States, creating an oil crisis in that country. Other countries, including Britain, were also affected by the embargo. Gas prices everywhere skyrocketed. The limited supply and high demand for oil led to gas rationing in many places. It also showed people the need to conserve energy. Slogans such as "Don't be fuelish" encouraged Americans to drive their big cars less often. It also encouraged car companies to build smaller, more fuel-efficient vehicles.

In 1973, drivers faced long lines at gas stations. Many stations ran out of gas!

■■➡ The Jaguar V12 engine gave the XJ-S some serious power. It could reach 60 mph (100 km/h) in just 7.8 seconds, and had a top speed of 142 mph (229 km/h).

XJ-S

In 1975, Jaguar introduced the XJ-S grand tourer. The XJ-S—which replaced the popular E-Type model—was a sports car with the sophistication of a sedan. The design of the car was dramatically different from the E-Type model. The XJ-S was less curved and more **aerodynamic** than the E-Type. The XJ-S had a very long hood, which was necessary to hold the car's massive 12-cylinder engine. At the time, only a few specialty car makers, such as Ferrari and Lamborghini, were using such huge engines.

Rear window

When the XJ-S was introduced in 1975, it was not an instant success. Buyers wanted smaller, more fuel-efficient cars, not gas-guzzling grand tourers. The car's design was criticized by some people, as well. The "flying buttresses" on the rear window raised safety concerns. A flying buttress is an arch that helps support the wall of a church or other building. It was the name given to the rear supports on the XJ-S model. Although the arched metal on the window strengthened the **chassis**, it also made it difficult for the driver to see out.

⟫ Flying high

In 1981, the XJ-S received a **high-efficiency** version of the V12 engine. Fuel economy of the XJ-S improved by almost 50 percent! The new engine boosted the car's sales. It also boosted its power output to 295 bhp. The XJ-S went on to receive numerous engine and design changes during the two decades it was manufactured. The flying buttresses—which were considered part of the car's character—remained on the XJ-S until it was discontinued in 1996, however.

The V12 engine of a Jaguar XJ-S. The model was later offered with the new AJ6 engine.

Vital Statistics

XJ-S

Production years: 1975–90
No. built: Approx. 88,000
Top speed: 142 mph (229 km/h)
Engine type: Jaguar V12 (1975–80); Jaguar HE V12 (from 1981); AJ6 I-6 (from 1983)
Engine size: 5.3-liter, 285 bhp (1975–80); 5.3-liter, 295 bhp (from 1981); 3.6-liter (from 1983)
Cylinders: 12; also 6 from 1983
Transmission: 4-speed manual (1975–78); 3-speed automatic (1975–90)
CO_2 emissions: N/A
EPA fuel economy ratings: 12 mpg; 16 mpg with high-efficiency engine
Price: Approx. US$18,000 (1976 model)

AJ6 engine

The AJ6 was the third engine designed and built by Jaguar. It was an inline six-cylinder piston engine that was introduced in 1983. The AJ6—which stood for "Advanced Jaguar six-cylinder"—was used by Jaguar throughout the 1980s and 1990s.

G76 WHP

Hard times

In the mid-1970s, a global recession occurred. The recession affected the United States, Britain, and many other **industrialized** countries. During the recession—which continued into the 1980s—many people were out of work. They could not afford to buy expensive luxury cars.

In the first five years of production, Jaguar sold fewer than 15,000 XJ-S models. A high-efficiency engine later boosted the car's sales to nearly 75,000 models in a ten-year period.

Killing the Spider

Responding to design criticisms, Jaguar hired an Italian car design company named Pininfarina to develop a new sports car. In 1978, Pininfarina introduced the sleek XJ Spider. The stylish grand touring **concept car** was never manufactured, due to financial reasons. Its design inspired future Jaguars, however, such as 1996's XK8.

⟫⟫ Money matters

Like many companies, Jaguar was affected by the recession. The company experienced financial difficulties and several ownership changes. In 1975, the British government **nationalized** the ailing company—that is, the government bought and took control of it. In 1984, Jaguar became a private company once again. In 1989, the Ford Motor Company purchased Jaguar.

Sign of the times

In the 1980s, compact, inexpensive cars ruled the roads in the United States. Chrysler's K-car series—which included Plymouth Reliant and Dodge Aries models—were huge sellers. Minivans also became popular. These large but fuel-efficient people-movers offered a practical and economical means of transportation.

Jaguar Land Rovers on the production line, while the company was part of Ford. Unfortunately, Jaguar Cars was not profitable for Ford and was sold in 2008.

Jaguar Cars became part of Ford's luxury line of automobiles, which also included Aston Martin, Volvo, and Land Rover brands. In 2008, Ford sold Jaguar to Tata Motors Ltd., a company based in Mumbai, India. The sale—which included Land Rover and Daimler marques—was priced at more than US$2 billion.

Project XJ40

In 1986, Jaguar introduced the XJ40. The refined four-door sedan had been designed to replace the original XJ6 model. It was delayed for several years, however, due to Jaguar's financial problems and the oil crisis in the 1970s. While it was delayed, engineers continued to test and improve the model.

Making the grade

The XJ40 model endured 1.2 million miles (two million km) of summer heat testing, 1.1 million miles (1.8 million km) of winter cold testing, and another 1.8 million miles (2.9 million km) of heat and dust testing! Jaguar invested more than US$300 million in the new model.

The project proved to be a worthwhile investment for Jaguar, as more than 200,000 XJ40 models were sold. Jaguar's extensive testing of the sedan also resulted in major improvements to the company's design and manufacturing processes. It was good all around!

By the time the XJ40 was built, it had become the most tested vehicle in Jaguar's history!

➤➤ Welcome to the 1990s!

The mid to late 1990s were a period of rapid economic growth in many countries. Unemployment was down and wages were up. People celebrated their success by spending money. They bought computers, cell phones, DVD movies, and other new technologies. They also began buying expensive cars again. High-end sports cars—like the popular Porsche Boxster and Honda NSX—offered high performance for a high price. Jaguar joined the party with the XJ220 supercar.

What a concept!

In 1992, Jaguar began selling the fastest production car that had ever been made. The Jaguar XJ220—named for its target top speed of 220 mph (350 km/h)—was a sports car with wings. The XJ220 prototype was introduced at the 1988 British International Motor Show. It featured a hefty 6.2-liter V12 engine, all-wheel drive, and scissor-style doors like those found on Lamborghini cars. Jaguar began taking advance orders for the stylish two-door sports car in 1989. With a deposit of US$80,000, interested buyers—which included Sir Elton John and the Sultan of Brunei—could place their names on a waiting list for the hot new car.

Supercars

The XJ220 is a supercar. Supercars are the fastest, most powerful, eye-catching, head-turning cars on the road. They have big engines—and big price tags, too! Lamborghini and Ferrari are some of the other companies that build supercars.

L2TWT

Production changes

When the production version of the XJ220 was revealed in 1991, however, major changes had been made to the car. It was offered with a turbocharged V6 engine, rear-wheel drive, and standard doors. The purchase price had also increased from US$580,000 to a whopping US$650,000! Some unhappy customers—who had signed contracts to purchase the original XJ220—sued Jaguar. Jaguar won its court battles, however, and went on to produce more than 280 of the restyled supercars.

■ The XJ220 was a mid-engine sports car—one of the most impressive Jaguars ever produced. But buyers had to part with US$650,000 to get one.

▲ The interior of the 1993 Jaguar XJ220R, an updated version of the fastest production car available at the time.

▶▶ The heart of a racecar

Although the XJ220 was built for road use, it had the heart—and design—of a racecar. The XJ220 was a mid-engine car, or one in which the engine is located behind the driver. The weight of the engine was spread over all four wheels, which improved the car's balance. Extra weight on the rear wheels also gave the tires greater grip and allowed the XJ220 to turn corners quickly. The XJ220 was also equipped with a roll cage. A roll cage is a strong frame inside a car that protects the driver from injury, especially if the car rolls over at high speed. Roll cages are usually found in racecars, not road cars!

The Saturday Club

In the early days of Jaguar Cars, a group of employees began meeting on weekends to discuss potential projects. They called themselves The Saturday Club. The idea for the groundbreaking XJ220 was created by this after-hours group. Jaguar liked the idea, and the XJ220 was soon put into production.

At The Saturday Club, Jaguar employees worked out every detail of the XJ220. This is the rear light cluster.

36

Vital Statistics

XJ220

Production years: 1992–94
No. built: 281
Top speed: 220 mph (350 km/h)
Engine type: Twin turbocharged V6
Engine size: 3498 cc (3.5-liter),
  542 bhp
Cylinders: 6
Transmission: 5-speed manual
CO_2 emissions: N/A
EPA fuel economy ratings: 21 mpg
Price: Approx. US$650,000

Wild and wide ride

The XJ220 was the fastest car ever made by Jaguar. It could go from 0 to 60 mph (97 km/h) in less than four seconds! It was also Jaguar's widest car, measuring almost seven feet (two m) across! The wide wheelbase allowed the XJ220 to turn corners at high speeds without tipping over.

Although Jaguar lost the title of fastest production car to the McLaren F1 sports car in 1994, the XJ220 remains a popular collectible car.

⟫⟫ XK8

In 1996, Jaguar unveiled the XK8 at the Geneva Motor Show. With its flowing, aerodynamic design and classic Jaguar styling, the grand tourer was, quite simply, grand. Under the car's classic long hood, the new Jaguar AJ-V8 engine sat ready to pounce. The powerful engine allowed the XK8 to reach speeds of 60 mph (97 km/h) in just 6.4 seconds. For safety reasons, the top speed of the car was electronically limited to 155 mph (250 km/h).

The XK8 was overflowing with thoughtful features, including a trip computer and power-adjustable heated front seats.

Fit for a prince

Available as coupe or convertible models, the XK8 was equally classy with its top up or down. With all-leather interior and genuine walnut trim, the XK8 set a new standard for comfort and luxury. In fact, an automobile journalist compared the interior of the XK8 to the inside of a British palace!

AJ-V8 engine

The Jaguar AJ-V8 engine is a dual overhead camshaft (DOHC) V8 piston engine. This compact but powerful engine was first used in the 1996 Jaguar XK8, where it generated 290 bhp of power. Since then, both standard and supercharged versions of the AJ-V8 engine have been used in Jaguar vehicles.

The XK8 became the fastest-selling sports car in Jaguar's history, admired for both its looks and its performance.

Rated R

The XK8 was available in a supercharged version called the XKR. This car was dangerously fast and glamorous. It was featured in the 2002 James Bond movie *Die Another Day*. The XKR in the film was particularly dangerous— it was fitted with door-panel rockets and front-grille machine guns!

Vital Statistics

XK8

Production years: 1996–2006
No. built: Approx. 91,000 (including supercharged versions)
Top speed: 155 mph (250 km/h)
Engine type: 4.0-liter Jaguar AJ-V8 (1996–2003); 4.2-liter Jaguar AJ-V8 (2003–06)
Engine power: 290 bhp (4.0-liter); 294 bhp (4.2-liter)
Cylinders: 8
Transmission: 5-speed automatic; 6-speed automatic from 1997
CO_2 emissions: N/A
EPA fuel economy ratings: 18 mpg (city); 25 mpg (highway)
Price: Approx. US$65,000– US$80,000 (convertible at higher end of range)

⟫ Executive decision

The Jaguar S-Type was revealed at the 1998 British International Motor Show. Borrowing its name from the 1960s S-Type, it was a stylish midsize executive car. An executive car is a spacious, elegant sedan that is often driven by successful businesspeople.

The S-Type was smaller and more affordable than the XJ model. It had a retro style, which means it was designed to look like a car from the past. Its features were decidedly modern, however. The S-Type was the first production car to include voice-activated controls, which allowed the driver to operate the S-Type's phone, audio, and temperature controls simply by speaking.

The original S-Type

The original S-Type sedan, produced between 1963 and 1968, is regarded by some as a design misstep for Jaguar. The sedan's rounded front end contrasted the sharp, sleek lines of its back half. A Jaguar engineer who helped design the first S-Type model admitted it was "an odd-looking car."

The X files

In 2001, Jaguar introduced the X-Type model. The X-Type was the company's first compact four-door sedan. It was an entry-level Jaguar that promised buyers affordable luxury. The X-Type Estate—a stylish **estate car** version—also promised a spacious interior and plenty of room for cargo. An estate car is a station wagon, or a passenger car with an oversized back cargo compartment. The X-Type Estate was the first production estate car ever to be offered by the luxury car company. The X-Type was also the first Jaguar vehicle to feature all-wheel drive. With so many firsts, it's no wonder that the X-Type was Jaguar's top-selling model at the time.

The X-Type Estate—called the "Sportwagon" in the United States—was introduced in 2004. It was the first estate to be offered by Jaguar.

During its final year of production, only about 900 of the original S-Types were sold—despite their obvious class!

41

Chapter 5

Racing Through Time »»»»»

Jaguar has a long and successful racing history. The speed, power, and agility of its high-performance cars have proven to be a winning combination. Although Jaguar has conquered racetracks around the world, it has been most triumphant at the 24 Hours of Le Mans.

Le Mans

Le Mans is an endurance race held in France each year. An endurance race tests the abilities of cars and drivers to complete many laps over long periods of time. Le Mans takes place on an 8.45-mile (13.6-km) circuit of closed public roads in a 24-hour period. It is the oldest and most prestigious endurance sports-car race in the world.

the race. Jaguar's successful record continued throughout the 1950s with C-Type and D-Type models. In 1988, Jaguar returned to the podium once again, celebrating a victory that was more than 30 years in the making.

Racing potential

Jaguar began competing in the Le Mans race in 1950. The company entered a team of XK120 cars in the race, and one finished in twelfth place. Sir William Lyons realized the car's racing potential, and Jaguar engineers immediately began modifying it for competition. The new C-Type model—originally called the XK120C—was ready to race the following year.

Built for speed

The C-Type model was built for speed, not comfort. It had no carpets, weather equipment, trunk, or exterior door handles. In fact, it didn't even have a passenger-side door! These items were unnecessary for racing and would have only slowed down the aerodynamic car.

Early wins

Jaguar's winning legacy at Le Mans began in 1951, when a C-Type car bested the competition in its first appearance at

The Jaguar C-Type was built for the racing circuit. From the 1950s, it competed in races such as Le Mans.

C is for competition

The Jaguar C-Type burst onto the race-track in 1951. Its name—which stood for "competition"—was chosen well, because this car was ready to compete! It had an aerodynamic shape, aluminum body panels, and a rigid, lightweight chassis. In fact, the C-Type was about 1,000 pounds (454 kg) lighter than the XK120 model. With a tuned-up version of the Jaguar XK inline six-cylinder engine, the C-Type had an impressive 205 bhp of power.

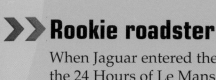

≫ Rookie roadster

When Jaguar entered the C-Type in the 24 Hours of Le Mans, few were expecting the rookie roadster to win. Three C-Types were entered in the race. Two cars dropped out with low oil pressure, but the third—driven by Peter Whitehead and Peter Walker— stayed in the race. The C-Type went on to win Le Mans with an average speed of 93 mph (150 km/h).

A winning investment

Only 52 Jaguar C-Type models were built, making them extremely valuable today. The C-Type originally sold for around US$6,000. Today, a 1953 Le Mans-winning C-Type car is valued at almost three million US dollars!

The C-Type began as a modified version of the XK120 and ended up being one of Jaguar's fastest and most successful racecars.

Le C-Type

In 1952, Jaguar was hoping for a repeat performance at Le Mans. Unfortunately, the modified C-Types that had been entered in the race proved too hot to handle. All the Jaguar teams retired from Le Mans with cooling problems. The following year, Jaguar returned to the C-Type's original design but added innovative disk brakes. Jaguar owned the podium that year, placing first, second, and fourth in the race! The winning C-Type—driven by Tony Rolt and Duncan Hamilton—averaged nearly 106 mph (170 km/h). It was the first car ever to achieve an average speed over 100 mph (160 km/h) in the endurance race.

The C-Type was the first Jaguar designed for racing. It drove the company to victory at Le Mans in 1951 and 1953.

Vital Statistics

C-Type

Production years: 1951–53
No. built: 52
Top speed: 150 mph (241 km/h)
Engine type: Dual overhead camshaft (DOHC) Inline-6 XK
Engine size: 3442 cc (3.4 liter), 205 bhp
Cylinders: 6
Transmission: 4-speed manual
CO_2 emissions: N/A
EPA fuel economy ratings: 12 mpg
Price: US$6,000

>> Jaguar D-Type

The D-Type roadster succeeded the C-Type—and succeeded on the racetrack, too! Introduced in 1954, the D-Type used the same powerful Jaguar XK inline six-cylinder engine as the C-Type model. The design of the D-Type was all new, however. Its long, tubular chassis was made from a single piece of aluminum alloy, which made it extremely strong and aerodynamic. The D-Type's construction had previously been used mainly in aircraft design.

■ Only 71 D-Type models were made from 1954 to 1957. In 2008, the first D-Type racecar ever made sold for more than US$3 million!

The D-Type's Chassis

Unlike other cars at the time—which were made with body panels covering a frame—the D-Type racecar had an innovative monocoque chassis. "Monocoque" is a French word that means "single shell."

Malcolm Sayer

Malcolm Sayer was a top design engineer at Jaguar. Sayer—a former aircraft engineer—was one of the first people to apply aerodynamic principles to cars. He designed the winning C-Type and D-Type racecars, as well as being responsible for the iconic 1960s E-Type sports car.

The Jaguar D-Type race-car won many races from 1955 to 1957, proving that it had both speed and staying power.

D is for domination

The Jaguar D-Type dominated the 24 Hours of Le Mans in the mid-1950s. Although Jaguar placed second to Ferrari in 1954, it was an extremely close race. In fact, it finished Le Mans less than one lap behind the winner—remarkably close for such a long race. The D-Type returned to Le Mans with a vengeance and went on to win the race the next three years in a row. In 1957, the Jaguar team won five out of the top six spots!

Ruling out the D-Type

In 1958, the rules of Le Mans were changed. Engines were limited to three liters in size. The winning D-Type model—with its powerful 3.8-liter engine—could no longer compete in the endurance race. Jaguar built competition D-Types with smaller 3.0-liter engines. The cars raced at Le Mans in 1958, 1959, and 1960, but they did not win. Jaguar stopped competing in the race and concentrated instead on making high-performance road cars.

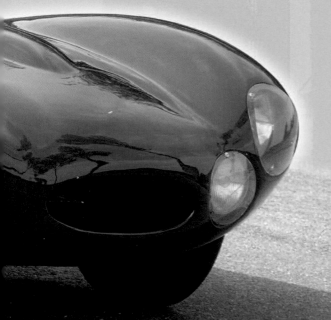

🏁 AMAZING FACTS

The ABCs of Jaguar

Jaguar's racecar series began with the letter C. There are no A-Type or B-Type models! This is because the C was meant to stand for "Competition."

>> Return to racing

Jaguar staged a comeback in the 1980s, returning to racing with the XJR series. The XJRs were low-profile racing machines with hefty engines and power to spare. In 1988, the Jaguar XJR-9 model won several important races, including Le Mans and another endurance race called the 24 Hours of Daytona. Two years later, the Jaguar XJR-12 accomplished the same feat, securing Jaguar's place in the world of racing.

Jaguar Racing

In 1999, the Ford Motor Company—which owned Jaguar at the time—purchased a Formula 1 racing team. Formula 1 is a highly regulated series of races involving the fastest and most technically advanced single-seat machines in the world. The Jaguar Racing team competed from 2000 to 2004. Although several Formula 1 champions—including Eddie Irvine and Johnny Herbert—drove for Jaguar, the team did not win any races. In 2004, Jaguar Racing was sold to Red Bull.

Vital Statistics

XJR-9

Production years: 1988
No. built: 6 (plus 2 built on the chassis of earlier models)
Top speed: 245 mph (395 km/h)
Engine type: 60-degree V12, mid-mounted
Engine size: 7.0 liter, 750 bhp
Cylinders: 12
Transmission: 5-speed manual
CO_2 emissions: N/A
EPA fuel economy ratings: N/A
Price: N/A

2010 Le Mans

In 2010, Jaguar returned to the 24 Hours of Le Mans with the RSR XKR GT2. The powerful new racecar is a 5.0-liter V8 with wings—or at least one large rear spoiler! Unfortunately, the Jaguar team was not able to finish the race because of engine problems.

▪▪➡ The XJR-9 racing at the Silverstone circuit, UK, in 2009.

! Mark Webber races for the Jaguar team at the Australian Grand Prix, in Melbourne, in 2004, the last year that Jaguar competed.

Jaguar XKSS

A few D-Type racecars were modified and sold as road models called the Jaguar XKSS. The XKSS was given practical—and necessary—additions, such as a passenger door and seat, a full-size windshield, and a basic folding top.

Chapter 6

▶Back to the Future ▶▶▶▶▶

Sir William Lyons once said that a car is "the closest thing we can create to something that is alive." Although Sir William Lyons no longer steers the company, Jaguar continues to fulfill his vision—to create beautiful cars that inspire, pamper, and impress. As Jaguar Cars Ltd. moves toward the future, it also honors its past and the stunning automobiles that drove the company to be successful.

Current models

Jaguar's current models combine the best features of its historic cars with the advanced technologies of today. Jaguar now offers three stunning cars—the sporty XF, the speedy XK, and the enduring XJ.

Jaguar XF

The XF is Jaguar's latest model. It was introduced in 2008 and became an instant classic. The XF is a midsize sports sedan, or a four-door car that handles and accelerates like a sports car. In fact, the speedy XF sprints from 0 to 60 mph

(97 km/h) in just 5.5 seconds! With the XFR high-performance 5.0-liter V8 supercharged engine, the time drops to a mere 4.7 seconds! The aerodynamic shape of the XF sedan helps it achieve such rapid acceleration.

Every part of the car—right down to its exterior mirrors—was designed to cut easily through wind. In fact, the XF is the most aerodynamic production car ever built by Jaguar.

The aerodynamic shape of the XF, launched in 2008 and still in production, makes it one of the fastest Jaguar models ever built.

One of Jaguar's most popular current models—the XJ.

Always original

"The development of our new range of cars is all part of making Jaguar the modern sporting company that it was under our founder Sir William Lyons—a company that made its name creating cars that were innovative, exciting, and always original."

Mike O'Driscoll, managing director of Jaguar Cars

>> Sporting luxury

The XF is one of Jaguar's most luxurious vehicles. The stylish sedan is designed for comfort and easy driving. With features like heated—or cooled—leather seats, heated exterior mirrors, and even a heated steering wheel, the Jaguar XF is hot! With a rearview camera, large in-dash touch screen, keyless push-button starter, and soft blue interior lighting, it is also extremely cool.

The innovative JaguarDrive Selector button, which is available on current models.

Vital Statistics

2011 XF

Production years: 2008–
No. built: Still in production
Top speed: 121 mph (195 km/h) XF/XF Premium; 155 mph (250 km/h) XF Supercharged/XFR
Engine type: 5.0-liter V8 (XF/XF Premium); 5.0-liter V8 Supercharged (XF Supercharged); 5.0-liter V8 R supercharged (XFR)
Engine power: 385 bhp (XF/XF Premium); 470 bhp (XF Supercharged); 510 bhp (XFR)
Cylinders: 8
Transmission: 6-speed automatic
CO_2 emissions: 264 g/km (XF/XF Premium); 292 g/km (XF Supercharged/XFR)
EPA fuel economy ratings: 16 mpg city and 23 mpg highway (XF/XF Premium); 15 mpg city and 21 mpg highway (XF Supercharged/XFR)
Price: US$53,000 (XF); US$57,000 (XF Premium); US$68,000 (XF Supercharged); US$80,000 (XFR)

Jaguar XK

The new Jaguar XK is the next step in the evolution of the XK series. The premium sports car—which replaced the popular XK8 model—was introduced in 2007.

Described by Jaguar Cars as "a grand tourer with the heart and soul of a sports car," the XK is both stylish and swift. It is a high-performance vehicle that can reach exhilarating speeds quickly. With an aluminum chassis and a top speed limited to 155 mph (250 km/h), it is the fastest of Jaguar's standard production models.

Twist and shout

The JaguarDrive Selector™ is an innovative gear twist knob that replaces a gear stick on Jaguar's latest models. The circular, metallic dial rises from the console with a touch of the push-button starter. A simple twist of the dial allows the driver to choose Drive, Reverse, or other transmission positions.

The XK, a premium sports car, was introduced in 2007 and has been tearing up the streets ever since!

>> A grand tradition

Available in coupe and convertible versions, the XK is also one of the company's most breathtaking models. The exterior of the car is both graceful and muscular. It features sweeping, athletic lines, a long front hood, a classic oval grille, and bulging rear-wheel fenders. Inside the XK, fine leather seats, wood veneers, and plenty of thoughtful touches make the XK as luxurious as it is powerful.

Happy anniversary!

In 2010, Jaguar marked its 75th anniversary with a limited-edition XK model—the XKR175. With an incredible top speed of 174 mph (280 km/h), and acceleration of 0 to 60 mph (97 km/h) in 4.4 seconds, the XKR175 is Jaguar's fastest car on the road today. Its aerodynamic design and large rear spoiler make it one of Jaguar's most stunning models.

The Jaguar XK—shown here in the convertible model—is truly a grand tourer in the grand tradition of sports cars.

↑ Car enthusiasts admiring classic Jaguars at a show.

Vital Statistics

2010 XK

Production years: 2007–
No. built: Still in production
Top speed: 155 mph (250 km/h)
Engine type: 5.0-liter V8 (XK);
   5.0-liter Supercharged V8 (XKR)
Engine power: 385 bhp (XK);
   510 bhp (XKR)
Cylinders: 8
Transmission: 6-speed automatic
CO_2 *emissions:* 264 g/km (XK);
   292 g/km (XKR)
EPA fuel economy ratings: 16 mpg
   city and 24 mpg highway (XK);
   15 mpg city and 22 mpg highway
   (XKR)
Price: US$83,000 (XK Coupe);
   US$89,000 (XK Convertible);
   US$96,000 (XKR Coupe);
   US$102,000 (XKR Convertible)

Generation XJ

The XJ has been Jaguar's flagship sedan for more than 40 years. The ground-breaking model set a new standard for luxury and performance when it was introduced in 1968. Since then, it has received numerous design changes and improvements. Today, the legendary XJ remains as stylish and innovative as it was when it first hit the streets.

Going clubbing

Some Jaguar owners belong to car clubs. They gather at shows and other events to share their stories, information, and, most importantly, their cars! Many car clubs produce newsletters and maintain websites that keep Jaguar owners—and those who wish they were—informed about both current and historical models.

▶▶ Staying power

The Jaguar XJ has staying power—and power to stay. This updated classic is available with a commanding 5.0-liter V8 supercharged engine that produces an impressive 510 bhp of power.

The XJ is as refined as ever, though. The elegant four-door sedan shares many of the same comfort features as the XF and XK models. With a large, spacious interior, however, the XJ has even more room for luxury. Options such as lighted rear vanity mirrors, rear business trays, and rear side window blinds offer passengers greater comfort and convenience. With a panoramic glass roof—complete with electric blinds—the sky's the limit for the heavenly new XJ sedan.

Jag-Z

The Jaguar XJ rocks! A 2011 model is featured in a music video by American rapper Jay-Z. In the video—for the song "On to the Next One"—the stylish XJ is used as a symbol of wealth and success. Now that's something to sing about!

The all-new XJ features vertical red tail-lights that wrap around the body of the car. The lights are designed to look like claw marks from a cat.

The sophisticated XJ, released in 2010, is one of Jaguar's most luxurious and comfortable models yet.

2010 XJ

Production years: 2010
No. built: Still in production
Top speed: 121 mph (195 km/h) XJ/XJL; 155 mph (250 km/h) Supercharged/Supersport
Engine type: 5.0-liter V8 (XJ/XJL); 5.0-liter V8 Supercharged engine (Supercharged); 5.0-liter V8 Supercharged engine (Supersport)
Engine power: 385 bhp (XJ/XJL); 470 bhp (Supercharged); 510 bhp (Supersport)
Cylinders: 8
Transmission: 6-speed automatic
CO_2 emissions: 264 g/km (XJ/XJL); 289 g/km (Supercharged/Super-sport)
EPA fuel economy ratings: 16 mpg city, 23 mpg highway (XJ); 15 mpg city, 22 mpg highway (XJL); 15 mpg city and 21 mpg highway (Supercharged/Super-sport)
Price: US$72,500 (XJ) to US$113,000 (XJL Supersport)

➤➤ Green machines

While Jaguar continues to reinvent its classic cars, the company is also looking ahead to the future and its impact on it.

Jaguar has been making environmentally friendly decisions for many years. In 2003, the company introduced a new, lightweight aluminum chassis on the XJ model. In 2006, the XK model was given an even lighter aluminum frame. These lightweight models use less gas than the heavy steel-bodied models of the past. In 2010, Jaguar introduced new fuel-efficient engines. With low CO_2 emissions, these engines are better for the environment. With more power than ever before, these new engines are better for drivers, too!

Giving back

Jaguar Cars is also trying to make up for the carbon emissions produced by its manufacturing plants. The company is investing in a variety of programs that help reduce **greenhouse gases** in the air. For example, Jaguar is helping fund a wind farm in Mulan, China. The farm—made up of 20 large turbines—uses wind power to generate electricity. Wind is a much cleaner energy source than coal, which is used throughout much of China. Jaguar also encourages drivers to compensate for their vehicle emissions by donating to this or other important projects.

Limo Green

Jaguar Cars is working on an exciting new project with the British companies Lotus Cars and Caparo. The goal of the project—called Limo Green—is to produce a full-size luxury sedan with low CO_2 emissions. To accomplish their goal, the companies are building a new **hybrid car**. The new, environmentally friendly vehicle will have an electric motor, a rechargeable lithium battery pack, and a small engine that drives a generator. With the Jaguar name on it, the hybrid car promises to have power—and style—to spare.

Forward thinking

As Jaguar drives into the future, it will continue to strive for grace, space, and pace in its automobiles. While the legendary car company celebrates its rich heritage and past triumphs, it is always moving forward and focusing on the future.

▪ Jaguar will continue to look for innovative ways to design and build high-quality, high-value cars that would make Sir William Lyons proud.

Jaguar Heritage Museum

The Jaguar Heritage Museum chronicles the company's remarkable history. Located in the former Jaguar factory in Coventry, United Kingdom, the museum features more than 150 exhibits. Jaguar vehicles, pictures, brochures, and artifacts tell the story of Sir William Lyons and the successful car company that he created.

Jaguar Timeline

1927   Swallow Sidecars begins making cars

1931   The SS1 model is introduced

1936   The SS 100 is launched

1945   SS Cars is renamed Jaguar Cars Ltd.

1948   The XK120 roadster is launched; Mark V sedan is introduced

1950   Jaguar begins mass-producing the XK120

1951   Mark VII launched; Jaguar takes its first win at Le Mans

1954   The first D-Type is unveiled

1955   Mark I sedan becomes a hit at home and abroad

1959   Mark II sedan is introduced

1960   Jaguar buys the Daimler Motor Company

1961   Jaguar introduces the E-Type Series I; Mark X sedan is launched

1966   Jaguar merges with British Motor Corporation; E-Type 2+2 coupe is added to the line

1968   Luxury sedan, the XJ6, is introduced

1969   The Series II E-Type is released

1971   The Series III E-Type joins the family

1975   XJ-S grand tourer is revealed; Jaguar is nationalized by the British government

1978   Pininfarina designs the XJ-Spider

1981   High-efficiency version of the XJ-S is introduced

1984   Jaguar is privatized

1986   The XJ40 is introduced

1989   Ford Motor Company buys Jaguar

1992   Jaguar begins selling the XJ220 supercar

1998   The S-Type is revealed at the British International Motor Show

1999   Ford creates the Jaguar Formula 1 racing team

2001   Launch of the X-Type

2007   Introduction of the XK model

2008   Jaguar is sold to Tata Motors Ltd.; the XF model is revealed

2010   Jaguar launches its 75th anniversary edition XK; fuel-efficient engines are introduced

Further Information

Books

Cars: Jaguar
by Michael Bradley
(Benchmark Books, 2009)

Ultimate Cars: Jaguar
by Rob Scott Colson
(PowerKids Press, 2010)

Blazers: Jaguar
by A.R. Schaefer
(Capstone Press, 2008)

Hot Cars: Jaguar
by Lee Stacy
(Rourke Publishing, 2005)

Jaguar: All the Cars (Second Edition)
by Nigel Thorley
(Haynes Publishing, 2010)

Web sites

www.jaguar.com
The official web site of Jaguar Cars Ltd.

www.jdht.com/JDHT/html/Trust/
Online home of the Jaguar Daimler Heritage Trust

www.jaguarmagazine.com/home.aspx
The web site of *Jaguar Magazine*, with all sorts of information
about the company and its cars

>> Glossary

2+2 coupe A sporty car with two seats in the front and two smaller seats—designed for children or occasional passengers—in the rear

aerodynamic Describing a shape that is designed to move easily through wind at high speed

alloy A substance consisting of two or more metals or of a metal and a nonmetal combined

chassis A car's frame

concept car A vehicle made to show a new design or technology

coupe A hard-topped sports car with two seats

drag racing A competition in which cars speed down a straight track

embargo A governmental law that does not permit trade with a specific country

estate car A station wagon, or a passenger car with an oversized back cargo compartment

exported When goods are shipped to another country for sale or trade

flagship The main model that represents a brand the best

grand tourer A two-seat sports car that is made for driving long distances in comfort

greenhouse gases Gases that trap heat in Earth's atmosphere and make the planet warmer

hearses Vehicles designed to carry caskets to funerals

high-efficiency Describing an engine that uses the least amount of gas for the highest performance

hybrid car A car that uses both a regular combustion engine and an electric system

iconic Referring to an object that is special or important, easily recognized, and which comes to represent a group or company

industrialized Countries that depend largely on the production and sale of manufactured goods

mass-produce To manufacture goods in large quantities, often using assembly lines

muscle car A high-performance, two-door car with a big, beefy engine

nationalized Taken over by the government—said of a once privately owned organization

opulent Very rich and luxurious

prestigious Important and impressive; notable for excellence

production car A vehicle that can be purchased by the public

prototype A test model

rationing The controlled sharing of a substance for which there is a limited supply

roadster A two-seat car that has no roof or side windows

sedan A passenger car with four doors and a back seat

sidecar A one-wheeled seat that attaches to the side of a motorcycle to carry an extra passenger or cargo

streamlined Having a smooth, sleek shape

supercar An extremely fast, powerful, eye-catching sports car

>> Index

Entries in **bold** indicate pictures